The
SACRED
APOLOGY

Other works in the Sacred Apology series
by Wayne Kealohi Powell

Reclaiming Original Innocence: The Way of Hoʻoponopono

The Truth Dialog: Embracing the Unlimited Self

By Wayne Kealohi Powell and Patricia Lynn Miller

Hawaiian Shamanistic Healing: Medicine Ways to Cultivate the Aloha Spirit (Llewellyn, 2018)

Visit the author's websites:

shamanicbodywork.com
waynepowellmusic.com
sacredapology.com
globalha.net

The
SACRED
APOLOGY

*Healing Cherished Wounds
through Compassionate
Self-Responsibility*

Wayne Kealohi Powell

Sacred Apology ∞ Book 3

The Sacred Apology: Healing Cherished Wounds through Compassionate Self-Responsibility © 2024 by Wayne Kealohi Powell. All rights reserved. No portion of this book may be reproduced in any form, stored in any retrieval system, or transmitted in any form by any means—electronic, mechanical, photocopy, recording, or otherwise—without prior written permission from the author, except as permitted by U.S. copyright law and fair use. For permissions contact: spirit@trustlove.us

First edition, 2024

Book design: Laura Berryhill
Cover design: Laura Berryhill

ISBN: 9798882677403

This work reflects the experiences of the author and is not intended to be prescriptive, nor an authority for medical or psychological advice. Should you require a doctor, always consult a licensed professional.

*To all teachers and practitioners of peace:
To all who strive for conflict resolution without violence;
To all who live as a true reflection of divinity, with
kindness, gentleness, and forgiveness;
To all who came to create and experience heaven on
earth—and to all who are learning to make it so.*

*To all who seek a more effective way to forgive,
a higher path to walk as the light of love,
and the freedom to be who they already are,
love in a body.*

I AM the Light of God that never fails;
I AM the Love of God that in all prevails;
I AM the Peace of God here to forgive;
I AM the Grace of God that forever lives.

−Kealohi

Contents

Contents vii
Preface ix
Series Introduction xi
Key Points 1
1: Preparing the Way................................3
   EXERCISE: Connect with Divinity, Reprogramming 1 7
2: Connection & Release 10
   EXERCISE: Connect with Divinity, Reprogramming 2 12
   EXERCISE: Practicing Innocent Perception 18
   EXERCISE: Releasing Pain & Tension through Observation 1 24
   EXERCISE: Releasing Pain & Tension through Observation 2 25
3: The Miracle of Forgiveness 30

  EXERCISE: Self-Treatment................................**35**
  EXERCISE: Self-Treatment with Our Ancestors.....**39**

4: Healing Masculine & Feminine........................49
  EXERCISE: The Masculine Practitioner's Role for the Feminine Receiver **64**
  EXERCISE: The Feminine Practitioner's Role for the Masculine Receiver..**66**

Afterword... 71

About the Author 73

Preface

Why and How to Read This Series

Most people have experienced an emotional wound or two at some point in their life. Sometimes those emotional wounds become associated with physical complaints, and stuck emotional complexes become aches and pains—or simply nagging patterns—that won't go away in the body. The good news is, these "problems" can be processed to become possibilities: they can set us on a course of discovery of who we are and the freedom to be our best self in our life and relationships.

Whether we are a healer or a receiver of healing, the Sacred Apology series provides guidance and transparency about the nature of our odyssey of discovery. It explores our life journey, unlocking and activating our personal and spiritual potential through the healing process.

The Sacred Apology series is intended to be read in order, and readers who start with a volume other than the first are encouraged to seek out the remaining volumes, as each of the three volumes offers a unique perspective and different insights into the healing process.

Some concepts are presented in discrete form while others are gleaned through immersion in the flow of the material. Main topics and exercises appear in an ordered progression to gently reinforce and build on previously encountered knowledge and skills. For easy reference, exercises are listed within each chapter in the table of contents.

This series is written with love from the perspective of several traditions that hold dear the idea that there is one benevolent source from which we all, and all of life emanate. Its major influences include Self I-Dentity through Hoʻoponopono, *A Course in Miracles* (ACIM), the original teachings of Jesus, and holistic spiritual science.

For more information on some fundamental components of the healing process, readers may enjoy referring to *Hawaiian Shamanistic Healing: Medicine Ways to Cultivate the Aloha Spirit* (Llewellyn, 2018) by this author—Wayne Kealohi Powell—with Patricia Lynn Miller.

Aloha, and happy reading.

Series Introduction

Understanding the Nature of a Healing Crisis: Healing as an Ongoing Journey

There comes a time in each of our lives when all that we think we know just isn't enough to get us through another day, when all the spiritual philosophy and training we've had isn't enough to overcome the chaos we're swimming in, when everything we've done before—that worked before—isn't working now. Instead, it actually holds us back from what we truly want to feel: whole, inspired, innocent, and free of the fear of being alone and not being enough.

For me, it felt like the passion that was driving my locomotive of desire had expired somehow. I came to an impasse and couldn't move forward. I saw clearly that all my attachments were holding me back from creating a new purpose for my life. As in childbirth, awakening and journeying through the birth canal can be a very intensely painful process. The empowered birthing mother is wise to breathe consciously through the most painful contractions, and then relax fully in between contractions to gather strength, back and forth, again and again, until an entirely new human being emerges. As a metaphor for self-renewal, *a whole new way of being emerges*. An ever-evolving, fully integrated, aware, personal–spiritual self arrives, beaming more primordial light into this world—illumination.

> *Full transformation requires from us that the will for radical change overcome our want and need for more of the same.*

Of course we know all this, but when it comes to truly living what we know we tend to back away from the discomfort of leaving our somewhat dysfunctional habits, thoughts, and behavior patterns behind. Could this be because we as humans are naturally driven towards pleasure, towards what is familiar, and away from pain or change? It may seem to our former self that a full transformation would cost way too much on every level of our life. Letting go isn't something we are trained in, and it doesn't always come easy to us. Life will take many people and things away from us, and yet through the grief we stubbornly cling to the past for a reference of who we are.

To start one's life over again takes a lot of courage. We may need to become shamelessly vulnerable and insecure, surrendering with blind faith to a source of power beyond our comprehension. When I reached this point, I had to trust that power to guide me through the darkest of times, allowing and blessing the grieving of the past, breathing myself through it into a new lifestream. I have reluctantly surrendered into this life-shattering death–rebirth process several times in this lifetime. It is always darkest and most painful right before the rebirth, when who-I'm-becoming begins to "crown" inside the cosmic birth canal. The me that was before is dying. In our weakest hour there's no reference for who we thought we were. We can only lay still in wonder about what form the new life may take. Then, all of a sudden, there's a strong pull-of-being from deep within, offering a spark of primordial light to usher us through the intense pressure of the expanding walls of the birth canal, out the other side, into the light, with a renewed purpose for living.

After our new self emerges the umbilical cord must be cut, totally unplugging the previous dependencies that held our life together. Every new lifetime (within this lifetime) has a clear beginning and a clear ending before the latest upgrade can fully engage its new abilities, with a greater capacity to serve the family of humanity with purpose and integrity.

These "lifestream upgrades" assist to cultivate a refinement-in-response to new challenges we will face. These challenges assist in promoting our soul's growth through a primal evolutionary process of maturing our capacity to love and be loved without conditions. A good analogy would be that when we get a new phone, our phone number remains the same yet the new phone's hardware and operating system have advanced capabilities. The new phone has the latest technology and new options for managing all our communications. There are many new features to learn about and more room for memory with so much creative potential. Welcome your new operating system, your new lifestream.

When leaving friends and family behind, the feeling of grief can be overwhelming sometimes. For me, the "laying down and dying" process is quite full-on and necessary, as I let go into the arms of a delicate, sacred, spiritual recalibration. It's as if I must allow the previous bonfire of my life that I built so meticulously, that was ablaze with passion, to completely die out. Then I can clean out the ashes before building a fresh new fire—a new life. Beginning again with dry leaves, dry kindling, and a few pieces of dry wood, divine fire—as personal passion—has a new creative expression.

A lifestream upgrade may appear as moving into a new place after a divorce; beginning a new job or career; starting a creative project or business that stimulates a burning passion for a creative expression; giving away old clothes; acquiring new clothes, or a different car or house; learning a new dance style, language, or musical instrument; or joining AA or a new exercise or study group of some kind, meeting new people and perhaps starting a new relationship. It could also involve letting go of a very lucrative income at a job we no longer have any passion for, in order to follow a more heartfelt career that nourishes our soul and serves humanity in a deeper, more harmonious and fulfilling way. In other words, we are letting go of old familiar habits, agendas, pathways, and people, and allowing our innermost being to advise us in creating a higher, more evolved version of our life with more purity of heart—one that is in alignment with who and what we are becoming.

Discovering or rediscovering who we really are is like finding a valuable treasure inside of us—or finally meeting our innermost being and falling deeply in love with our angelic nature as our new best friend. We didn't even know our own being was here for us, let alone that it was possible to have a "live-in" companion who will always love us unconditionally, within all circumstances. These are life's most precious and exciting times: growing through all the challenges into serendipity, synchronicity, and the joyous wonder of feeling totally in love with our whole self; witnessing, walking and talking as keen awareness; breathing in infinity with ecstatic wonder of the great mystery.

Mystics often say that we are born into each lifetime for a specific purpose that gives our life meaning, and that within each lifetime we are given specific gifts to fulfill our soul's purpose. Yet we tend to get caught up in living a life that we didn't seem to choose, a life that was chosen for us by our parents or by our teachers and preachers. How do we find out who or what we really are? We ask questions such as Who am I? What am I? To whom or to what do I belong? Why have I come here? What is my purpose for living, right now, in this moment? Who, what, why? What do I believe in that may be holding me back?

A spirit-guided inquiry such as a *truth dialog* has always worked for me to crack open these questions and let in some light. Finding honest answers through prayer and meditation that come from our deepest heart's longing will serve our highest and best interest. The truth dialog begs for core-splitting honesty to reveal and uncover the authenticity of our soul's magnificence and reboot its original blueprint for an inspired life filled with meaning and purpose. This activation brings fulfillment only through witnessing the pain and joy of all our choices here, from moment to moment, while allowing our innermost being to guide us.

The games of the unconscious mind are many. Most of them look socially playful and somewhat harmless—until they hurt us deeply by activating our cherished wounds, challenging our beliefs and social morality about what's right and wrong, acceptable and unacceptable. Greed and misuse of sexuality seem to be the major moral offenses of our time. Our moral boundaries were put in place to protect us. From a viewpoint of higher consciousness one might ask, protect us from what? From ourselves? From being hurt and hurting others? From feeling our own darkness so we won't project it onto others? From our aversions to what feels bad, and our cravings for what feels good? From our human foibles and mistakes? Or from discovering that we are actually love-in-a-human-body, and this comes with huge responsibility?

Our experience of good or bad is merely showing us our beliefs and our preferences manifesting consciously or unconsciously. Carefully witnessing how our programming affects our feelings will assist us in reclaiming our free will to seek healthier pathways for our precious energy to flow into our personal and spiritual evolution with more grace and less resistance.

Our thinking, calculating mind dwells on the past and the future while our sacred heart lives in direct vertical communion with the timeless being that dwells in every cell of our body. It harbors all the qualities that we attribute to divinity—it is a sacred portal through which we can engage and experience our immortality. This is what keeps the sacred heart pure. And this is why we "go vertical" to connect with divinity for meditation and for processing life's challenges. When we align vertically with spirit, spiritual law activates and responds, assisting us to delete the old painful narrative. What happens next often appears as a miracle—a flow of divine love cascading from just above our head down into all our bodies—goodness overflowing once again through all aspects of our life.

Serendipity and synchronicity have reappeared to create a whole new experience of life. Thank God.

Let me remind you that love is a state of being, not a feeling. Peace is not a feeling. Joy is not a feeling. These cherished feelings arise as "fruits of being," cultivated from living in harmony with spiritual law. Feeling deeply loved, peaceful, and joyful are states of being that we cultivate very consciously and carefully from being fully aware that God is always present, living within our chaotic mind and physical body. Pure consciousness is living with us, as us, and for us.

The experience of living in this new awareness or perception becomes the spiritual practice of constantly witnessing, accepting and modifying all chaotic thoughts, beliefs, and misunderstandings—the base metals—into gold and silver. Then we, as awareness, arrive on a higher perch, embodying a more being-filled experience, transforming the "doing" of mistakes into lessons learned, through the eyes of the angel that we are, witnessing our humanness.

I sincerely encourage you to muster the courage to navigate through the minefield of conditioning and unforgiven hurtful experiences in various relationships. A sacred apology just might be the holistic medicine you've been longing for to rebalance, recalibrate, and harmonize all your relationships, especially the one with your own primordial light. When body-mind and soul are in alignment with spirit, the heart opens wide and all becomes possible. Tears of joy will flow as our vulnerability becomes easier to manage through the grace of a blessed life consciously lived.

As we close our eyes and dive deep within, with profound tenderness, we find a quality of pure awareness that we long for and perhaps didn't know existed—within a quieted, still heart. Let's explore this delicate, gentled aspect of our heart together with a willing, open mind. Our heart knows the truth of our existence as infinity alive in every cell of our body. Let us begin an inquiry to transform our wounds into possibilities, honoring what habits need to die, mature, and evolve for us to upgrade our experience of life on earth—a life that awaits our welcome. As we devote ourselves to living our full potential as love in a body, this practice will shower us with infinite blessings of divine and human love, beyond all conditional limitations.

Welcome to the rest of your life.

May all beings be happy,
Wayne Powell, D.D.

Key Points

The Sacred Apology: Healing Cherished Wounds through Compassionate Self-Responsibility

- *Practicing mind-body-spirit connection to prepare for healing the past*
- *The nature and format of the sacred apology*
- *Achieving innocent perception*
- *Self-healing via the sacred apology; healing others*
- *Healing with the divine masculine and feminine: perspectives on polarity to achieve unity*

The *sacred apology* teaches us how to become self-responsible and self-reliant in all our human relationships. It reminds us to *go vertical*, retraining the mind to see every event as neutral and everyone in an event as innocent. When we go vertical with our breathing and sincerely apologize to our higher self for each of our human transgressions and hurtful interactions with others, grace will relieve our guilt, shame, jealousy, and hatred. From this divine perspective all is forgiven. Within this self-responsible role modeling, the truth sets us free of the past!

In healing sessions, the *truth dialog* and sacred apology are used to clear the way for divine healing in all our bodies. When love, light, and harmony have been restored to their rightful place within our body-mind complex, our experience of bodywork will be more effective, longer lasting, even permanent. Permanent change requires the healing journey to address the physical, mental, emotional, volitional, and spiritual bodies—all aspects of the whole self. This is truly holistic medicine.

1
Preparing the Way

The sacred apology is a revolutionary forgiveness concept and process that I explored and developed over many years of teaching *hoʻoponopono* one-on-one and in larger groups. It is an effective form of spiritual confession, restoration, and rejuvenation. It can bring us back into harmonious emotional balance, liberating us from the deep imprints that may arise from living our lives through the filter of personal issues: prejudice, resentment, jealousy, abuse, abandonment, lack-consciousness, and hatred.

The necessary encounters of living offer us the experience of fully feeling our feelings. Our feelings can teach us how to discover and observe the beliefs and expectations that are their root cause. Someone else is not the cause of our feelings. When we become responsible for what we feel, which is generated by our own subconscious mind, who is left to forgive besides ourself?

The cosmic light we all come from—God, universe, primordial light—is always ready, willing, and able to assist us in letting go of memories of harmful mistakes that harbor guilt, shame, tension, and pain.

Preparing and Opening

In order to facilitate a sacred apology successfully it is wise to cultivate a love for life in all its manifestations, along with an intuitive ability that can be trained to respond to every trauma or drama with loving compassion. Doing this work for ourself first—practicing how to "go vertical" and uplifting into the *spirit channel* our need to be right—is so important. Letting go of our own cherished wounds is a prerequisite to helping others do the same.

Once we have a deep appreciation for a working relationship with our *soul cluster*—body-mind-spirit—we can reclaim our innocence and enjoy living our life. Others in our presence will be able to recognize and reclaim their own innocence, and in turn see it in others. This is the best starting point—innocent perception is impersonal, yet all encompassing—a divine perspective heals.

A quiet room, where we would normally meditate or open prayers, mantras, and blessings, facilitates a sacred apology most effectively. An altar with sacred tools, as well as pictures of deities and family members, can assist in focusing our reverent attention. True freedom is the goal of all spiritual seekers, but the layers of shame, blame, and resentment that we all carry are not easily undone. We can find wisdom in learning how to carefully observe our thoughts, witnessing how they orchestrate our life and all our communications within our relationships. The power of spirit to make us whole again within this forgiveness technology has absolutely no limitations. It can heal the most broken relationship on a deep inner level.

Self-identity ho'oponopono requires us to assume full responsibility not just for our own actions, but for everyone else's actions as well. While this level of responsibility may sound a bit extreme, when we look more closely we discover that what we see in the world is reflected through our own filtered programming. We are seeing only what we have learned to believe. This makes us completely responsible for all that we see! What everyone is doing, or what we think they have done, belongs only to us.

Once you carefully ponder the following four statements and let them alter your thinking, you will begin to see things quite differently. They represent the psychology of "true vision" from a perspective that has no limits and is purely innocent and self-responsible.

When you change the way you think about something, the something you think about will change.

–Wayne Dyer

Nothing I see in this room [on this street, from this window, in this place] means anything.
—*A Course in Miracles Workbook*, Lesson 1

I have given everything I see in this room [on this street, from this window, in this place] all the meaning that it has for me.
—*A Course in Miracles Workbook*, Lesson 2

I do not understand anything I see in this room [on this street, from this window, in this place].
—*A Course in Miracles Workbook*, Lesson 3

When we fully absorb the implications in the above principles at the deepest level, we will understand what self-responsibility really is. Only then will we be ready to accept full responsibility for what we think we see, because we're only seeing what we have been taught to see—nothing more, nothing less. When our perspective changes, what we see changes.

Through the eyes of divinity everyone is always innocent, regardless of what we think has happened. This spiritual law opens the way for us to discover and accept what we were taught to see, and retrain our minds to view all that we see through the eyes of the angel that we came here to be.

Now, let's prepare our space and our body-mind for sacred communion with divinity. Let's light a few candles and cuddle up in bed or in our favorite cozy reading chair. Or we can sit on our meditation pillow. We are about to embark on a journey of healing so profound that our toes will curl because our mind will soon stand down from stubbornly holding onto the need to be right, from self-righteous beliefs and judgments, and from telling hurtful stories repeatedly, reinforcing their false validity. There is another way.

We will now endeavor to open the spirit channel and call on divinity for assistance with this healing process. As we begin, we allow whatever emotions may arise to just be with us on the journey. They will shift and change once we get underway with the process.

EXERCISE: Connect with Divinity, Reprogramming 1

Make yourself comfortable and close your eyes. Now, imagine that there's a waterfall of divine, cosmic light just above you, pouring down into the top of your head and energizing your body. See if you can feel this golden light pouring into you from above, and generate gratitude for it.

Now, imagine that this light is more intelligent than you could ever comprehend. This light loves you unconditionally and sees you as completely innocent, no matter what you think of yourself.

Now B-R-E-A-T-H-E, very slowly and vertically—up and down, from just above you, down into your belly. Offer your love and gratitude to this light for sustaining your life. As you B-R-E-A-T-H-E vertically, slowly, deeply, feel this golden light pouring into every cell of your body as pure cosmic particles of God. These are healing sparks of creative Intelligence—adamantine particles. They are commanded by love into form, from infinity.

You are going to repeat the proclamations below out loud to yourself over and over for one full minute. Set your watch. Breathe in light from above very deeply and slowly before stating each proclamation. Then, state the proclamation while exhaling, directing it into every cell of your body, here and now. Focus on F-E-E-L-I-N-G it land in every cell, creating lots of happy cells as they absorb the frequency of cosmic light entering each and every cell of your blood, bones, and flesh.

Now, B-R-E-A-T-H-E, very slowly and vertically—up and down, from crown to belly. Speak directly to your soul's light and proclaim each statement out loud as you exhale:

I AM ONE WITH YOU...	I AM
I AM LOVED BY YOU...	I AM
I AM LOVING YOU...	I AM
I AM LOVABLE...	I AM

Repeat these four lines over and over, out loud, for one full minute using the formula above, breathing in golden light, until you *feel* what you're saying fully root within your body-mind complex and your psyche.

After this meditation you may feel called to be still for a while, to enjoy the peaceful, easy feeling this quality of work brings you. This exercise can be repeated as often as desired or required.

2
Connection & Release

There are many types of healing that allow the past to be laid to rest. The sacred apology is a simple yet profoundly healing ritual that can open the heart to the abundant love waiting on the other side of truly forgiving ourself for the most hurtful thoughts, words, and actions. We can't change what's been said. But we can change how we feel about it now—changing how it affects us for the rest of our life.

The sacred apology's primary function is to liberate us from useless thought-forms, relative truths, and hurtful memories that keep robbing us of our joyful coexistence with one another. It can be used in a clinical or casual setting if the space is sanctified and both parties, giver and receiver, desire a sincere resolution. It can also be used alone in the privacy of our own home, heart, and mind.

Sacred apology is rooted in ho'oponopono, an ancient form of conflict resolution from Hawaii, that's been around since humans discovered the need for this kind of healing for their families. Our present-day use of this form of healing has changed to delineate a very specific and unique style of forgiveness that takes a new shape for the consciously awakening ones of today and for those of us who wish to share the clear spiritual perception that God holds for each soul in a body.

In order to understand how a sacred apology works, it serves us to examine the nature of perception, projection, and the mechanics of judgment. Let's continue to look at how we form our expectations of life around what we believe to be true; then let's examine how our expectations in turn create and reinforce the judgments we hold toward everyone and everything.

We have become so accustomed to judging everything without even knowing we are doing it—including events, everyone we meet, friends, family, strangers, plants and animals, the weather—that we actually don't have a reference for life without some form of personal interpretation or judgment. And yet, judgment is at the root of all hurtful words and actions and is the primary cause of all forms of reaction, war, and disease. Almost everyone's doing it, all the time. Many of us know that the antidote to judgment is forgiveness, but we really don't know how the mechanics of a true letting-go work. However, as we learned in the truth dialog, going vertical and calling on divinity for resolution can and will assist us to become more open and free.

Forgiving someone doesn't condone what they have done. It merely sets us free from the karmic ripples of holding a negative feeling toward someone and harboring self-righteous anger or guilt because of it. Our forgiveness allows the *law of cause and effect* to deal with the other person, while we are spared from holding poisonous, negative feelings toward another inside ourselves.

EXERCISE: Connect with Divinity, Reprogramming 2

To prepare: Locate in your mind what you hate about someone you have loved deeply. Is there something about the way they speak to you or what they say that drives you to anger? The keys to this exercise are first, decide you don't want to be angry. Second, decide you want to know why they trigger your anger response. Once you've made these decisions, you are ready to receive the answers.

To engage: Make yourself comfortable and close your eyes. Now, imagine that there's a waterfall of divine, cosmic light just above you, pouring down into the top of your head and energizing your body. See if you can *feel* this golden light pouring into you from above and generate gratitude for it.

Now ask your higher self why you get so triggered when this person says certain things to you. Just listen deeply from a still mind and open heart.

Then ask your higher self when *you* have said or acted the way they do toward you. Sit quietly and listen carefully with a still mind. Allow your higher self to bring you a memory of a time when you did or said something very similar to trigger someone. Listen with an open mind like a good detective, to discover when you acted in this way. Perhaps you're being this way now with them and can't see it? When you see clearly that you have been like the one who triggers you, this can be an "aha" moment of revelation.

You will repeat out loud to yourself the proclamations below, over and over for one full minute. Set your watch. Breathe in light from above very deeply and slowly before stating each proclamation. Hold the person you dislike in the light as you breathe.

Now, begin. B-R-E-A-T-H-E, very slowly and vertically—up and down, from crown to belly. Speak directly to your soul's light above you and proclaim each statement with confidence:

I CHOOSE TO SEE THIS DIFFERENTLY...
(breathe deeply 3 times)

I CHOOSE TO FEEL THIS DIFFERENTLY...
(breathe deeply 3 times)

Repeat these lines over and over, out loud, for one full minute using the formula above, breathing in golden light until you *feel* what you're saying fully root within your body-mind complex and your psyche. You are watering the truth and shifting the energy within you.

After this meditation it may feel best to be still for a while, to enjoy the peaceful, easy feeling this quality of work brings you. This exercise can be repeated as often as desired or required.

Perception & Projection

In spiritual psychology perception is generally considered a feminine attribute and projection masculine. Perception is what a baby does all the time—it perceives scents, sounds, colors, sizes, and shapes of things and catalogs that information as a reference for remembering what it's looking at. Perception is the assimilation of incoming data through our six senses: touch, taste, feel, see, hear, and sense. This is how we learn and categorize. We observe our experience through sensory awareness, and note what we observe: fire feels hot, water feels wet, wind feels cold or dry, stones feel hard, etc.

Projection, on the other hand, is the process of applying an arbitrary meaning that we were taught, to someone or something: a good/bad man or a good/bad idea, or a good/bad cook. To project is to assign a definitive interpretation, to form an opinion about something or someone, to give it/them a personal value.

Yet, in the realm of spiritual science all things and events are absolutely neutral. They have no meaning, as we learned in the previous exercise. Therefore, what we project onto someone is merely created from our moral and societal programing—it's simply what we have been taught to believe about something, someone, or some kind of behavior. Judgment and comparison are rooted in separation thinking—us and *them*.

The irony of projection is revealed by the childhood axiom, "It takes one to know one." Spiritual science has discovered that the perceiver cannot see in another what doesn't exist within themself. In other words, we can only see in someone else what already exists within us. In this way, we are always seeing an attribute of ourself, externalized and projected onto someone else. This axiom is true especially if we don't like what we see, if we're in denial of a particular quality also existing in us. We simply project what we don't like within ourself onto another. Then we accuse or blame the other for it. None of this will make much sense to a mind that is deeply rooted in feeling like a victim and is accustomed to blaming the world and others for its experience of life. A new paradigm is awakening in millions of souls who prefer to be sovereign and free.

Our projection onto someone prevents us from seeing that what we're judging in them also exists within us. All the while we are actually judging ourself, as them. This way of "perceiving" is rooted in *unity consciousness*. In truth, if we are not innocent, no one else will appear innocent. On the other hand, if we can't see others as innocent, then we are not innocent either. We are all connected intimately through the *one spirit*. We are many variations of one theme—cosmic consciousness, embodied.

When we see innocence, for example in a little baby, it brings a smile because it reflects the truth of our own original innocence. No one judges a baby unless it's quite noisy and annoying—then someone will project upon it because the baby has awakened the noise going on in their own head, that they were unaware of.

Innocent Perception

Those who sincerely undertake the advanced course in forgiveness, learn to view everyone they see as a reflection of themselves—they disengage from automatic judgment-reaction responses. The spiritual practice of innocent perception takes many years to master because the human mind is a relentless judgment machine. When we decide to change how we see things, the mind does not give up its program of judgment easily. It takes a strong will, determination, and consistent discipline to make any progress toward seeing everyone as innocent and all events as neutral. Yet, this practice brings us into alignment with divine perception as an impersonal witness of the world's chaotic appearance, offering us a peaceful coexistence with all of nature and its inhabitants.

The journey of innocent perception begins with a spiritual awakening to one's own innocence and a firm decision to perceive everyone else as innocent—no matter what the ego reads into what *appears* to be. The "flip-it" exercise in the truth-dialog process is the best way to deal with the mind regarding our habitual judgment responses. When judgment arises, we can gently guide our mind into changing our view into the opposite of what we're thinking. After we've done this, what we see now begins to glow and our feelings of separation disappear. We experience a oneness with what we are seeing, and a reunion with what is—polarity resolved.

Jesus states in Glenda Green's book, *Love Without End: Jesus Speaks*, that "separation is the original sin."

In the practice of innocent perception we are training ourselves to see others the way we are perceived by God, and the way we want them to see us—as healthy, although imperfect, free beings, doing our best, living and working through our human challenges.

The feeling of being accepted by others is vital for our healthy coexistence. It is a primal longing we are born with—to belong, to feel safe, and to be accepted for who we are. Innocent perception is a practice in remembering to go vertical, which enables us to view everyone, including ourself, from a much higher perspective—as a perfect, radiant being, having a physical, often emotional, experience through the minefield of our conditioned beliefs and expectations.

In the advanced course on forgiveness, there's only one person to forgive, ever—ourself—for judging ourself or another as less than perfect. All is perfect when viewed through the eyes of an angel. We each have the ability to be an angel in our human form and view life from this perspective, on demand. The practice of innocent perception brings us into alignment with sacred vision—the awareness and experience of seeing divinity within everything and everyone. Innocent perception is a complete liberation from creating hurtful consequences (karma) through judging or resenting ourself or another.

EXERCISE: Practicing Innocent Perception

This exercise builds upon the four statements we pondered in Chapter 1. It is based on the three statements from the workbook of A Course in Miracles (ACIM).

Nothing I see in this room [on this street, from this window, in this place] means anything
–ACIM Workbook, Lesson 1

I have given everything I see in this room [on this street, from this window, in this place] all the meaning that it has for me.
–ACIM Workbook, Lesson 2

I do not understand anything I see in this room [on this street, from this window, in this place].

–ACIM Workbook, Lesson 3

When done diligently this exercise offers us an experience of innocent perception.

To prepare: sit quietly, anywhere you are comfortable, and close your eyes. You could be in a park or in your bedroom. It won't matter where if your focus is strong. Go vertical with relaxed breathing and let your mind settle into your breathing until you feel very relaxed and calm.

To engage: Repeat, one at a time, all three statements until you believe or feel what you are repeating become reality in this moment, in your body-mind.

As you breathe, repeat this line three times and wait until a shift has occurred—until you believe or feel what you are repeating become reality in this moment, in your body-mind—before moving on to the next line:

Nothing I see in this room [on this street, from this window, in this place] means anything.

Again, as you breathe, repeat this line three times and wait until a shift has occurred before moving on to the next line:

I have given everything I see in this room [on this street, from this window, in this place] all the meaning that it has for me.

Finally, as you breathe, repeat this line three times and wait until a shift has occurred before opening your eyes:

I do not understand anything I see in this room [on this street, from this window, in this place].

Now, slowly open your eyes and notice something in your environment like a chair, a table, a door, a glass or cup, something that doesn't seem alive. Immediately release your mind from any thoughts or concepts about what you're staring at. Imagine firmly that you have no idea what it is, or what it's for. Stay with it until the object has absolutely no meaning to you. Hold this perception for as long as you can, like a baby does, in wonder of what it is.

Now, imagine that this object is present, here, with you to serve your life in some way, one piece of the puzzle of your perceived environment. Go deeper into not knowing what it is and continue to stare at its beingness, just sitting there, quietly, with no agenda.

As you continue to perceive it without meaning, it will naturally begin to glow. As the template of its physical data becomes revealed to you, you will see or feel a soft faint aura of light around its shape. This auric glow is its presence, as perfection. It is living the purpose it was created to be—to be present, as love, in service, just like the sun, the moon, the stars, and the whole of the earth.

Remembering Our Divinity

Most people come for healing to discover or reclaim their personal power. They inwardly long to remember and feel that they are not victims of the world. The hurtful challenges we experience on the physical plane are necessary for personal and spiritual growth. These opportunities arise only to boost our problem-solving abilities as we develop or improve our intimate, healing relationship with divinity as the predominant provider and controlling factor in our lives.

Once we have reconnected with our being, a vertical realignment takes place automatically within our soul cluster, our body-mind-spirit complex, and the experience of health can now regenerate itself. We, or our client, may still have some physical pain, but reconnecting with our divinity will always bring a more peaceful experience to the most painful life circumstances.

Once a vertical engagement has taken place within our soul cluster we simply are no longer alone in our misery. It becomes lighter and more manageable because we have shared it with and given it to a higher authority for resolution. Now our experience of life will reflect this in joyous and wondrous ways of personal fulfillment on every level of our being. This shift changes everything. The awareness of divinity that surrounds us and resides within us, when called into action, offers us grace, harmony, and peace during all our human challenges.

Feeling the Emotions Fully, Without Resistance

Pain, when experienced fully, consciously, without protection or blame, creates vulnerability and humility. When we accept full responsibility for creating the consequences of our misperceptions, then pain becomes our teacher and we can experience it as a personal growth exercise, kind of like working out at the gym. At this point, suffering becomes an option.

When we allow any kind of pain to fully flower within our body-mind complex without resistance, it can show us the limiting beliefs that played into creating the painful circumstance. When we learn to allow and *relax* the body while the pain is happening, without any resistance, the thought-forms causing the suffering and holding it in place will begin to let go of us. Trying to diminish the pain is a form of resistance to it and will always bring more tension, along with some form of suffering, as the pain fights back. What we resist, persists.

Pain is fire. It has the power to heal. Only when we resist growing pains in any form, does pain naturally become suffering. Childbirth reveals this so elegantly. Transcending labor pains by simply allowing each painful contraction to swell and then diminish, opening our hearts wider and deeper than the physical discomfort, seems to be the best way to process intense pain.

We can use conscious breathing to employ a powerful loving resilience—an impeccable unity with divinity to relax within painful contractions. When pain is allowed to flower unimpeded, something entirely new is given the space to be born into this world and assume its rightful place here. Once the baby is out it has a life of its own, which is again subject to the limitations of the material world. Without resistance, love has overcome fear within a birthing process, and now something new exists in the world. That's a miracle! Miracles will show up every time we learn to *trust* divinity and *allow* it to heal what appears to be happening to us.

It hurts a lot when our fantasies, misconceptions, moral beliefs, and romantic delusions begin to unravel, unwind, and burn up in the fiery furnace of unfulfilled expectations. Being very still within the pain will most effectively allow it to pass with more ease. Just witness, do not let the mind engage the pain in the usual way.

Many people who come for healing have found their miracle through only the truth dialog and sacred apology, without receiving any bodywork. The absolute truth will always set us free when we allow it to become our default healing tool for the misery before us.

A client came to see me for shamanic bodywork because she was carrying back and shoulder pain. She understood the opportunity that a truth dialog and sacred apology hold because she had experienced it before in other sessions. She sat in a chair across from me throughout the truth dialog inquiry, emotionally clearing and cleaning a few relationships issues that had become painful for her. We could both feel the knots unraveling in her body-mind as she changed the way she perceived others, which allowed her to relax and reclaim her power. Together we enjoyed the healing trance of profound forgiveness—sharing in the bountiful blessings that a clear mind and clean heart will always offer us.

After opening and forgiving several of her deeply hurtful misperceptions she felt so totally received, relieved, and inspired that she got up from the counseling chair and stated that she didn't need a massage anymore, that her physical pain was completely gone. She thanked me profusely and left. She was glowing gently with a lightness of being that she had not felt in a very long time. The truth had indeed set her free from the pain and tension she had arrived with.

EXERCISE: Releasing Pain & Tension through Observation 1

This exercise will assist in reprogramming your mind's relationship with any tension or pain you may be experiencing.

To prepare: Sit quietly, anywhere, at home or in a park, and relax deeply with your eyes closed. Notice your breathing and just relax into it, allowing your body to become quiet.

To engage: Now tune into all the sounds around you without allowing any interpretation of what you hear enter your mind. Just breathe and relax. Notice any tension or pain that your body may be holding onto. Scan your body very slowly and carefully: one arm, one leg, one shoulder, one hip at a time. If you are in pain, it will be obvious where to place your attention.

Practice *attentive listening* (see Sacred Apology Book 1, *Reclaiming Original Innocence*, for attentive listening exercises) with your body, moving from part to part. When you find the tension, hover over it with attentive listening and just observe it and breathe. Don't try to change it. Just observe it, in wonder, and listen to it care-fully, without interpretation. Be still and just observe. When you feel a shift, the tension unwinding, just let it go without doing anything. Watch, breathe, and let go.

EXERCISE: Releasing Pain & Tension through Observation 2

To prepare: Sit quietly, anywhere, at home or in a park, and relax deeply with your eyes closed.

Notice your breathing and just relax into it, allowing your body to become quiet.

To engage: Place your attention on the top of your head, just above you. Open your attentive listening skills and begin very slowly moving around your head. Observe care-fully as you spiral around and down, slowly, from your head to one of your shoulders. Now spiral slowly around the shoulder and down the arm, observing the elbow and wrist areas. After reaching the hand and fingers, go to the other shoulder and do the same.

Now return to the top of your head and begin again, this time spiraling down and around the head, then around the whole upper torso, very slowly. If you come upon any tension, hover over it for a second or two and just observe and breathe, nothing more, no agenda!

When you complete the upper body area, begin spiraling down one leg beginning at the hip, and do the same as you did with the arms, slowly moving around the thigh, knee, calf, ankle, to the foot. Just observe and breathe as you spiral. When you come upon tension or pain, hover, in wonder, with no interpretation, and listen deeply for no reason at all, just to be present fully with your body. Now do this again with the other leg from the hip down.

After you have completed a full-spiral scanning of the entire body, one part at a time, you are ready to begin again above your head with a new pattern. This time, spiral down the whole body from head to toe in one, slow, spiraling sweep. Begin again above the head, very slowly spiraling around the head and neck, down around both shoulders and upper chest, down around the whole upper torso including both arms, then the hips and belly, both upper legs, the knees, and lower legs to the feet.

Repeat as desired. This is a pure cosmic cleansing through observation, in wonder, witnessing how our focused, loving attention is a powerful healing tool when used without any agenda, just to observe innocently what is before us, and breathe.

Energy, presence, and love will always flow to where you place your attention.

Surrender to the Process

It takes great courage to open the memories and emotions that we have locked up inside. With a sincere heart-centered approach, with a truly willing self or client, many things can be forgiven, untangled, and resolved in a relatively short time. That's why we always honor all feelings that may arise. We welcome them, along with their hurtful memories, into the current of relaxed acceptance that we have provided for them in the sacred healing environment.

The sacred apology is a dialog that uncovers the absolute truth buried underneath our hurtful memories—that exposes the issues that are being triggered by others. These others appear out of nowhere and unintentionally poke at our tender wounds, bringing our awareness to what and who needs forgiving—now. For us, there are only two kinds of forgiveness: now, or later. Which will you choose?

A Course in Miracles states: *What is real* (permanent) *cannot be threatened*; *What is unreal* (impermanent) *does not exist*. The truth that is true always is the great dissolver of embedded, crystallized feelings from hurtful imprints and trauma being held within a story containing an emotional charge. We can use a potent forgiveness ritual to uncover what is *real* for ourself or our receiver. We can witness the dissolve of yucky blockage, like a potent drain cleanser freeing up the flow of energy once again.

Consciously focused, intentional breathwork can also trigger the release of stuck, blocked emotions. Screaming, yelling, and banging of pillows is common during a conscious breathwork or rebirthing session, giving underlying feelings an open avenue of expression for release, with volcanic fervor if necessary. The negative charges that were perhaps buried in another lifetime may have carried over to this one for another chance at resolution. Our soul evolves and matures in this way, lifetime after lifetime, remembering its perfection as we heal our separation thinking.

3
The Miracle of Forgiveness

Sacred apology can be used first for our own personal healing. Below we will explore how we can clean our mind of expired contracts with ourself and others, releasing any *undefined unforgiveness*—you know, the emotional baggage that we drag around and dump onto others so that we can see it more clearly. Undefined unforgiveness hurts us and the other. It can only serve us if we can see it as a reflection in the other, own it, and reframe it as "impersonal." If we take it personally, we will suffer.

Conflict with another is just "data" running through a program in our mind, that collides with another person's data, running through a program in their mind. Everyone carries different data from different personal experiences in life. When we view the world from what our memory shows us, we will only see our past projected onto the world and all our experiences. Then we try to make the world, or the person, conform to what we would prefer to see, so that we'll be more comfortable being with them.

This way of dealing with relationships is quite common, yet fragmented. Reacting from separation thinking only produces more suffering in the end. Opinions often collide, and then people wind up in a debate or an argument. Through the spiritual practice of innocent perception, we will see each person as light-in-a-body having a human experience. Judgment can serve the purpose of showing us what program is running in our own mind. From here, we can accept full responsibility for our own programming, and this will soften our one-sided, biased point of view, making it less rigid, more impersonal. Now we can allow the other's opinion and not react with unkindness. Everyone is entitled to their own point of view. Each person's opinion is simply a relative truth for them. The absolute truth needs no defense; it has no polarity. It is whole and complete.

The self-treatment sacred apology is an encapsulation of a delicate forgiveness process done alone with one's being or higher self. The process is streamlined for those who are already doing some form of ho'oponopono and getting results. This version of the sacred apology is designed to increase our ability and effectiveness in the art of letting go of a cherished wound, to reveal everyone's innocence within the story.

How this process differs from other forms of ho'oponopono is in the protocols of going vertical, and breathing and cleaning with divine light, the compassionate eraser for all imagined errors.

A Safe Container

As practitioners, shamans, ministers, bodyworkers, mystics, and artists who facilitate healing, it is vitally important to create a safe container for the sacred apology to be implemented. The quieter the space, the less noise, the deeper the healing can go into our psyche. Almost all of my experience with this work has been in healing temples, before doing any bodywork. This is also a wonderful practice to do alone, every day upon waking, and before going to sleep.

Containing the energy keeps us safe from any outside influences hindering our focused attention. Being in the quiet environment of our own home or some other kind of sanctuary is extremely helpful in facilitating a strong connection with our spirit, mind, and body. Our trifold being often requires an environment of stillness for transcendence. Sacred space can be anywhere that we feel safe being emotionally vulnerable. It could be anywhere where others can't see us or project upon us. Then our heart can relax and begin to open.

How It Works

From a cosmic point of view, we are the crown of creation—the fruit of all star-seeded universes. When we cultivate an intimate relationship with God, and that relationship has become fully conscious within our body-mind-spirit complex, then we can access instant healing more effectively in our daily life. This relationship can be fairly easy and without effort, although cultivating it does take a lot of trust and practice. To access our higher wisdom, we will breathe vertically. "As above" becomes "so below," as we overlay the frequency of heaven onto our earthly experience.

It helps to have a spiritual guide through the minefield of our beliefs and conditioning—one who knows the human mind well and can help us navigate through resolving our cherished wounds without blowing ourselves up. My guide is my divine being—the light of my soul—residing within and around me, rooted in my sacred heart and extending into the cosmos. Most of our soul's radiance lives just above our body; there's just too much cosmic light to be compressed into the physical container of a human body.

When we go vertical, a sublime access to our higher self, our being, opens up. With our eyes closed, we visualize our energy center just above the top of our head as a portal that opens wider, to assist more golden-white light to enter all our energy fields and various bodies. As we breathe vertically into our self-forgiveness ritual, we are prepared to release thoughts and feelings that are crimping the flow of our love.

No one deserves to suffer. We were not created to suffer. We can transcend the relentless pain and discomfort life offers us with conscious breathing and letting go of all that is not love or loving. Though not easy sometimes, it can be very simple.

As we drop into a meditation prayer and connect deeply with our being, we speak the apology directly into the light above us—activating a sincere and humble giving up of the hurtful feelings we are harboring towards ourself or another. By letting go of our engagement with unconscious programs that create melodrama, we are willingly releasing what hurts us. I'll say that again. By letting go of our engagement with subconscious programs that create melodrama, we are willingly releasing what's causing our suffering.

Basically, we are apologizing for our inability to be kind and loving toward ourselves and others all the time, within all circumstances. This process is a very healthy daily practice. And it feels very much like a personal, intimate, confession—a full activation of a spiritual cleansing. Doing the process at bedtime is a very effective practice. After a good cleansing and clearing of our feelings, judgments, and projections before dreamtime, we will sleep more deeply, more peacefully, and wake up with a renewed fresh start, ready to greet the day.

EXERCISE: Self-Treatment

To prepare: As I recall how I've hurt others and how I've have fallen short of being loving and kind all the time to myself, I choose to let these thoughts and feelings go once and for all.

I pray to begin the process, acknowledging the unified field within spirit, mind, and body, closing my eyes and opening my heart for divine intervention and resolution. I desire resolution with my whole heart and soul.

To engage: I call in light from above my body to enter through the top of my head, descending into my belly as I breathe it in fully.

As I breathe it in, I connect with and feel these particles of light as a subtle warm glow expanding within me.

I continue to breathe deeply, vertically, as I prepare for a verbal cleansing with divinity above me, within me, and around me.

After several deep breaths I begin to share and confess each of my hurtful thoughts, actions, and words to divinity with a sincere apology for the hurt I've caused myself and others.

I breathe in deeply three times between each apologetic statement while uploading my dense feelings into light. With each apology I am cleaning, clearing, cleansing, erasing those memories.

I apologize to my body for allowing these toxic memories to be stored there for so long as to create some form of suffering.

As I continue to forgive myself for carrying the guilt, shame, and blame for these errors I feel relieved; a gentle, warm compassion consumes my perceived errors with light. I use my breath to carefully move the light into where the memories were being stored.

As my feelings are lifted into grace, I respond to this divine intervention with gratitude, and my body is so relieved of holding these memories. Sweet liberation!

I joyfully say *thank you, I love you* to divinity, and then to my body for letting go. I feel so loved by light. It is easy to feel gratitude for this grace, as I feel so much lighter, cleaner, free of the gravity that was holding me down.

The Self-Confession Process

As we breathe in light, the light pouring downward, in through the top of our head, our eyes closed, we open our heart and go vertical—breathing in golden-white light from above. Then we say out loud what we're declaring forgiveness for. Not asking, declaring! There's no need to ask spirit for forgiveness because divinity has no capacity to judge us for what we think we've done, thought, or said. Divinity holds the view of innocent perception, always.

We choose this humble dialog of truth with pure conscious light for surrendering our human feelings that cause misery within our body-mind complex. These thoughts and feelings arise from our moral and societal programming, which does not allow any peace of mind or freedom of heart to fully authenticate within us. Rigid belief systems offer too much limitation for an open-minded person.

Here are some examples of what to apologize for:

I apologize for the way I treated so-and-so;
I apologize for what I said to so-and-so;
I apologize for not loving and accepting myself more fully;
I apologize for thinking I'm unlovable or not enough;
I apologize for acting self-centered, self-righteous, and arrogant;
I apologize for trying to manipulate so-and-so;
I apologize for trying to rescue my spouse, child, parent, or friend;
I apologize for my harsh judgments and control dramas;
I apologize for making the coffee too strong;
I apologize for drinking way too much;

I apologize for playing small in my life;
I apologize for not having the courage to go after my dreams;
Etc.

Whatever our apologies are, we want to always remember to B-R-E-A-T-H-E deeply from our belly—our feeling center—up into the light above us, while uploading each declaration into divinity's warm, receptive embrace. Divinity's clear, resilient radiance is like a cauldron of divine fire and will envelop, digest, and transmute the negative feelings back into nothingness. We can use divine light as our laser-beam eraser for our misunderstandings and moral mistakes that are not loving or kind.

If we approach divinity with humility and a loving sincerity, with no worldly agenda for anyone else, the process works—every time—to relieve any feelings of guilt, shame, or blame. In this way, the process is truly a work of art manifesting as a personal-confession prayer of redemption. When we are kind and loving to ourself and others, we feel lighter within us. Love is the feeling of holy divine light moving through our spirit-mind-body soul cluster. May the source be with us, always and all ways.

I find this personal confession with divinity quite habit forming because I feel so free, existing within a lightness of being, when I let spirit do the work and allow it to fully bloom within. It feels so good, that when the process is complete, I must consciously choose to refrain from clinging to spirit as my personal savior—even though it is. Instead, I invite infinite love to become my best buddy, manifesting within and around me, visiting me as often as I need it, the consummate lover within all life.

There is one more aspect of the self-confession process that deserves our attention. An added way to do this process is with an awareness of our ancestors being present with us. When we invite them into this ceremony to participate, we may find and experience a sort of communion with them. You see, we carry in our blood and DNA what they could not resolve in their lifetimes. This also suggests that the self-confession process may be reversed, allowing our ancestors to apologize to us for what remains in our bloodline that they could not evolve when they were here.

EXERCISE: Self-Treatment with Our Ancestors

To prepare: As I recall how I've hurt others and how I've fallen short of being loving and kind all the time to myself, I choose to let these thoughts and feelings go once and for all. As I address these human issues that I carry, I invite my ancestors to join me. As they enter, I recall aspects of my own behavior that trigger others that I have relations with. At times, I can act arrogant, self-centered, condescending, controlling, manipulating, and insensitive. And I wonder how and why I got this way, as I look toward my lineage.

I pray to begin the process, acknowledging the unified field within me connecting me with my ancestors, closing my eyes and opening my heart for divine intervention and resolution. I desire resolution with my ancestors now and I invite them to enter the circle of forgiveness that I have formed for this purpose.

To engage: I call in divine light from above my body to enter through the top of my head, descending into my belly as I breathe it in fully. Then I call one or more of my ancestors to join me in this self-confession ceremony, asking them if there's anything they would like to apologize for, that resides in me because of them.

As I breathe in whatever I hear them say, I listen carefully for their apology to me and feel their warm compassion for the challenges they have left me with. I then imagine that they acknowledge me for being willing to evolve these lower human qualities, as I learn to clear and clean what was left in the DNA for resolution.

As I continue to breathe vertically and feel their sincere apology entering my body-mind complex, I connect with and feel uncountable amounts of adamantine particles of divine light, filling me with a subtle warm glow expanding within.

I continue to breathe deeply, vertically, as I acknowledge what's occurring, a cleansing with divinity above me, within me, and around me for and from my ancestors.

After several deep breaths I begin to share and confess each of my thoughts, actions, and words to my ancestors with a sincere apology for the hurt I may have caused them by continuing to repeat their behavior.

I breathe in deeply three times between each apologetic statement while uploading my dense feelings into light. With each apology I am cleaning, clearing, cleansing, erasing those hurtful behaviors in my bloodline.

I apologize to my body for allowing these toxic memories to be stored there for so long as to create some form of suffering in myself and others.

As I continue to forgive my ancestors for carrying guilt, shame, and blame for these errors, I feel relieved; a gentle, warm compassion consumes their perceived errors with light. I use my breath to carefully move the light into the spirit of my ancestors.

As my feelings are acknowledged as being food for my ancestors and lifted into grace, I respond to this exquisite process with gratitude. My body feels so relieved of holding these lower human qualities for my ancestors. Sweet liberation!

I joyfully say *thank you, I love you* to divinity, and then to my body for letting go. I feel so loved by light. It is easy to feel gratitude for this grace, as I feel so much lighter, cleaner, free of the gravity that was holding me down.

Our Angelic Nature

Being bathed in the presence of our "angel within," the one who knows what is wise to say and do in every situation, leaves us feeling loved by life itself. This connection and experience can be practiced so that it occurs in all human circumstances, under all conditions, as a default application. We can download it into our human biocomputer and into our psyche and then practice, practice, practice innocent perception. When we practice it often, emotional swings will not be as deep and wide and will occur less and less often as we grow our angel wings.

Within all human encounters, we all are in training to respond to life more like our angelic being than our human being. Releasing the negative bad habits of our ego thinking will allow a mature romance with our own angelic self to fully bloom. Once this transformation takes place, there's no turning back. The end of suffering is clear and accessible, anytime, anywhere. We become a transparent presence observing life as an aware witness, not reacting, shining light onto all we observe.

Identifying ourselves with our humanness is rooted in the idea that we are our body, our job, our religion; we are the roles we play, such as father, mother, sister, brother, uncle, aunty, teacher, student. Yes, we do have a body, and we do play roles, but those things are not who or what we are. We are stardust—carbon-based units—designed to hold cosmic light in residence and experience ourselves as honorable stewards of this beautiful blue planet, living in perfect harmony with each other, caring for one another. We have the capacity to learn from each other through our errors and choices. We discover what is righteous, and what isn't, by way of all our feelings in harmony with spiritual law.

In doing this practice daily, from moment to moment we can cultivate an upgrade—a higher-frequency operating system within our psyche, offering us a deeper joy and peace that shows up in all our relationships. A peaceful lovingkindness is the byproduct of this spiritual practice. Shift happens! In *ACIM* Jesus states, "I need do nothing" (to be free of suffering). When we allow and observe in the same way the sun does, just radiating, requiring no compensation of any kind, we will overcome separation, becoming weightless to the gravity of human suffering.

Practice Devotion with Discipline

Anyone can download this "application" and run the program in their biocomputer. It takes devotion to run the application successfully and lots of consistent—daily—practice. But it's worth it. The end of suffering is at hand. We can be fully present with any challenge and be a still observer in the eye of the storm, feeling our emotions fully, while witnessing the storm come and go. After running the new program during an intense emotional encounter, the way we feel will inform us how well we are doing with our new spiritual practice. Our new perspective will invoke divine compassion for ourself and others. In each experience throughout our day, we will choose to view the drama from above, looking down upon our life like we're watching a good movie full of drama, romance, action, and suspense.

For many years I have witnessed young and old alike doing this practice and creating much harmony where there once was chaos, pain, and confusion. They have simply learned to go vertical, activating the program of self-responsibility with a truth dialog, and then using a sacred apology while breathing in light to erase hurtful stories. This practice is potent frequency healing, bar none. When we bring light to what is dark within us, it will always have an effect on everything and everyone in our life.

Opening in total vulnerability with deep humility in communion with God has elicited profound releases for so many. We tend to hold ourselves away from clearing with another because we are afraid of confrontation. We instead default to a belief that "time heals all." This thought-form requires time for healing to occur—sometimes lots of it. A miracle requires no time at all for an instant healing to occur. The "time heals all" idea becomes a convenient way to avoid verbal communication of our feelings. But suffering will continue until our distorted, unhealthy thoughts and hurtful feelings have been released in a healthy way. Many people having issues with another strive at all costs to avoid verbal communication and being outside their comfort zone. Yet, spiritual science states that until forgiveness has completely healed our mind of separation thinking, no peace or compassion will be able to fully root and bloom within us.

The sacred apology is the best way to counteract this avoidance program because we don't need to confront anyone else to heal our own hurtful issues *now*! Guilt, shame, jealousy, resentment, and blame can be resolved with a sacred apology in several minutes, in the privacy of our own home, at our prayer altar, in communion with our angelic self—instead of taking hours, days, months, years, or lifetimes to let go of what's holding us away from feeling loved and being loving, free from identifying with the melodrama.

Our mission—should we choose to accept it—is to end our suffering and pay it forward by assisting others to end their suffering. This spiritual healing will shift the frequency of the entire planet Earth and our personal lifestream into operating more fully within spiritual law, enhancing our wellbeing and peace of mind. Our heart will learn to stay open through all emotional upsets and within all the challenging situations life offers us, truly a worthy pursuit for anyone growing into more light and desiring to learn and share an effective technology for self-healing of their precious, cherished wounds.

The Buddha repeatedly said "May all beings be happy." He knew that his teachings would end the suffering of anyone who applied his teaching correctly. He knew that all he had to do to keep himself clean and clear was to share this technology with others, because we teach best what we most need to learn. So, I encourage you to learn this practice well and then pay it forward. Share it with all the ones you care for, and everyone else you encounter. We learn best through example.

A Horizontal Application of the Sacred Apology

The sacred apology is taught primarily as a vertical application because through it we employ divinity to relieve ourselves of anything unclean in our body-mind complex. Yet, the sacred apology can also be used horizontally through a gestalt dialog between healing practitioner and client. The horizontal application of sacred apology is subject to human interaction, judgments, and beliefs, whereas the vertical process is not.

Normally, when we apologize to someone for a wrong that we've done, our ego is invested in the other person forgiving us. When this is the agenda behind our apology, if they don't forgive us, we feel worse. That's why the sacred apology process is primarily invoked vertically, with divinity, because divinity sees only our innocence—that there is nothing to forgive. This perspective is the best start because we are in training to learn it when viewing others. Within this perspective, we have nothing to lose but the feelings that cause us suffering.

When a client is heavily invested in giving or receiving an in-person apology from someone, the practitioner can use this in the client's favor, by playing the role of the other person. The practitioner, as the other person, can either apologize or forgive them, as the need presents itself. The practitioner can make it *feel* real, by acting on behalf of the person the client is needing to forgive or receive forgiveness from. If the client is apologizing to someone, wait to reply to the client's apology until they have completely fulfilled their need to apologize, saying everything they came to say, then reply sincerely as the other person: "I forgive you."

Of course, it works both ways. Sometimes the receiver is seeking an apology from an offender that abused them when they were much younger. In this case the practitioner would again be acting a role as the offender in this scenario, humbly listening to the receiver's story. The practitioner, as the offender, listens carefully and waits to respond until the whole painful story has been fully expressed. Then, the practitioner, as the offender, may deliver an apologetic reply.

Healing polarities using the sacred apology will be detailed in the next chapter.

4
Healing Masculine & Feminine

Restoring Balance between Masculine & Feminine

The sacred apology can heal trust and safety issues between men and women, restoring divine right order within the matrix of a unified field. It is often used as a universal forgiveness protocol for the collective spirit of all masculine, as *one man*, and the collective spirit of all feminine, as *one woman*.

In ancient times in the culture of Hawai'i, they had one name for the spirit of God. It was Kanewahine. *Kane* means man. *Wahine* means woman. This reference to God proclaims man and woman as two aspects of one being. Kanewahine acknowledges that the masculine and feminine principles together signify inseparable polarities in union. The Chinese did the same with Yin and Yang. Two sides of the same coin.

It took a physical mother and a physical father to bring each of us into a physical body. Spirit and matter are the inseparable counterparts of the respective masculine and feminine aspects of all created form. This interrelationship is how both feminine and masculine energy exists within us regardless of physical gender. Therefore, keep in mind that what you see in the outer world that appears out of balance between men and women also exists within each of us. This is why, when we see an injustice against the feminine or the masculine, we feel so uncomfortable.

Men are born with the right and the privilege to be masculine—the principle, or source of power, that feeds energy to the feminine principle of creation. The masculine force (through both genders) goes to war, defending what it believes in, while feminine grace (through both genders) repairs and nurtures the soldiers when they return. The profound value that a balance between the sexes holds is not taught to us when we are young, growing into adulthood. As young boys we may have felt a prompting to excel at sports—a poor replacement for the traditional rites-of-passage found in aboriginal cultures. Our culture is in dire need of men who know the protocols for becoming mature and trustworthy husbands, protectors, fathers, and providers as well as authentic, kind, and generous gentle men, and in some cases, great warriors.

Women are born with the right and the privilege to be feminine—the receptive aspect of the androgynous light of creation itself. Goddess power has been growing more prevalent in public awareness since the 1960s, when the women's liberation movement began to take hold. There are more and more "goddesses" appearing lately, teaching our budding youth culture the protocols of becoming empowered and sovereign women, mothers, daughters, and nurturers. In recent decades many women have entered into and excelled in the corporate world, including all forms of sports and the military. For centuries there have been women leaders running countries all over the world.

At the highest level of a mature masculine and feminine union, all of creation supports the balance of these primal polarities—peace within equanimity. The conscious union of the polarized masculine and feminine forces celebrates the dance of spirit and matter coexisting within the limitations of a mortal life. This life is the paradox: immortal beings choosing a very temporary existence here on earth to learn about love and fear, separation and unity. Life offers our soul's yearning a variety of experiences to fulfill its purpose here, remembering the truth in being the love we are through all the ups and downs of the human emotional rollercoaster.

Unveiling the eternal truth of love divine as our source of existence is of utmost importance in our world today.

People of any gender may not experience full emotional maturity if they are unable to cope with or process their cherished wounds with someone trustworthy and skilled enough to assist their heart to open, let go, and heal.

If we choose to be more feminine in a man's body or more masculine in a woman's body, no matter: the balancing of both feminine and masculine matrixes within our collective field of embodied consciousness remains the same. The sacred apology addresses the imbalance we inherited from our ancestors very effectively. It is not gender specific, it is universal, offering us liberation from all polarized memories, known and unknown. After a thorough clearing, we arrive at the middle way, witnessing ourself as the most perfect, human imperfection.

The Need for Spiritual Evolution

The deepest imprints of betrayal and abandonment can carry forward through lifetimes when left unresolved. This need to restore divine right order and balance between the masculine and feminine is one good reason we return to earth. We are here to heal, to remember, to recover our whole, authentic self, and to learn to walk in and as light—the timeless within time—as love, under all conditions: "…through the valley of the shadow of death, I will fear no evil."

Anyone may carry ancestral wounds from mothers, fathers, spouses, sisters and brothers, from within this life or another. Within the ritual of sacred apology, healed women are able to sincerely respond and listen to the injured masculine psyche that feels unsafe with certain women who trigger him. Healed men are also able to sincerely listen and respond to the injured feminine psyche that feels unsafe not only with certain men, but also with some of her most beloved and challenging sisters. Broken men are often healed within a forgiveness ritual through a woman's soft, compassionate, open heart. And traumatized women are often restored to their full strength and wholeness within a forgiveness ritual through a man's gentled, tender, compassionate heart.

This healing can bring to both giver and receiver a better, more authentic understanding of how forgiveness actually takes place between the masculine and feminine counterparts of our seemingly complex existence. When balance has been restored and gender prejudice has been lifted, this profound healing creates strong, whole men and women with wise, open hearts. They become the seasoned practitioners who can feel and understand the whole gamut of another's painful cherished wounds. More and more great healers are showing up in the world today. They are the courageous ones, who've healed their cherished wounds that triggered reactions from unresolved issues.

The sacred apology has infinite applications for anyone willing to share it. Our beloved Earth requires this quality of loving attention at this time regarding the abuse of her body—the mountains, forests, jungles, lakes, rivers, streams, oceans, and wildlife. Through exploitation and degradation of our natural resources, we are choking off our very existence here on earth. We can offer Mother Earth an ongoing sacred apology from and with our cosmic father to accelerate her imminent healing.

Healing Authority Issues and Control Dramas

Healing our parental authority issues plays a huge role for both genders in how we relate to all others, be they teachers, bosses, coworkers, parents, children, government officials, preachers, or significant others. No one likes being told what to do or how to do it. It feels condescending and disempowering. For most everyone, the damage shows up in the form of authority issues and control dramas.

When we enter puberty, we begin the journey of self-discovery, separating ourselves from our parents and all expressions of definitive authority. Some of us never grow out of this rebellion. Whenever we feel any arrogance from others who think they know what's best for us, it becomes a force that drives us into a search for our own way. This issue can become lifelong, triggered when anyone wants to control our actions for any reason. This dynamic is the most primal one that needs maturing in the masculine/feminine, father/mother, parent/child dyads. The sacred apology can be used very effectively for healing this issue when guided specifically, intuitively, and attentively.

Dissolving Our Own Projections

As the receiver tells their story, we can go vertical and clear the energy within and around their hurtful memory by allowing it into our own energy field and clearing our own feelings and projections about what we are hearing. As holistic healing practitioners, we can assist everyone's forgiveness process by forgiving (clearing) our own projections onto the receiver as they share their painful memories with us. As we bathe the receiver in waves of light-filled innocent perception, it will enable them to let go of their projections and release the hurt being held within their body-mind complex.

Preparation for Healing

Women are the keepers of the culture, the family, the home, as well as the foundation of the world. The lesson that the women have to teach the men is how to be gentle. It's the women who are going to change the world now, and so the men have to protect them. The men need to follow the women for a change, because in doing so, men will become more selective. It's about

discrimination, about learning discernment. This is Mother Earth, it is not Father Earth. The energy of the earth is feminine, it is about Haumea, and the lesson for the men is about gentleness. The job of the women is to teach the men how to be more gentle. So, it's time for the men to sit down and listen, and it is time for the women to stand up and speak.
–Hank Wesselman, *The Bowl of Light*, "Hawaiian kahuna, Hale Makua speaks"

The divine feminine is growing stronger in our world at this time and the sacred apology is a wonderful key for opening women's and men's hearts for this healing to proliferate with grace. Again, because the sacred apology can heal trust and safety issues between men and women, restoring divine right order to the unified matrix, it is often used as a universal forgiveness protocol for the collective spirit of all masculine as *one man*, and the collective spirit of all feminine as *one woman*.

There is only one masculine and one feminine source materializing as the one spirit within many forms. That's why the issues that require healing appear in reflection with more than one person. Over time, an unhealed issue will resurface again and again through several different people until it has been healed and the emotional charge has been completely lifted. All are liberated when the memory has been drained of its toxic reactionary capacity.

For thousands of years, women have been raped, suppressed, and dishonored by men. The earth has also been raped, abused, and misused by unconscious masculine force. Many women today still feel deeply traumatized, hurt, and unsafe in the world, and they are carrying this pain for the earth, for their sisters, and for their ancestors. An emotionally traumatized woman will naturally hold back her love from a man that she feels unsafe with. Withholding is a way of defending herself from being controlled or dominated and hurt again. Yet withholding love perpetuates the looping of resentment, and the war between the sexes.

As gentle men who love and honor women, we may feel deep compassion for the divine feminine. We can clearly see a golden opportunity for both men and women to clear this unconscious, forceful energy from our past, present, and future. We may not be able to change the past, but we can change how we feel about it in the present in order to heal the past, preventing it from being dragged into our future.

A healed masculine is a force that can play a profound role in the healing of the divine feminine; a healed feminine is a nurturing power that can play a profound role in the healing of the divine masculine. Each person's heart and emotional body cries out for an intimate, authentic experience of their whole self, free of negative feelings, held and loved as a sacred being. The practitioner can hold and contain sacred space for a receiver who is truly willing to forgive the deeply buried wounds from hurtful masculine–feminine transgressions that have been embedded in their psyche, perhaps for generations.

In the sacred space of the healing temple the deepest ancestral wounds, carried within the receiver's body-mind may be recalibrated, laying to rest those hurtful memories, healing those deep imprints, uncovering and restoring the receiver's original innocence—a healing so profound it resonates to the core of our mother Earth and allows healing to take place on many levels for the entire human race.

When a woman chooses a male practitioner in order to heal specific issues with disturbing men, or a man chooses a female practitioner in order to heal specific issues with disturbing women, it fosters the release of hurtful memories and feelings of mistrust and disrespect that are imprinted on that person's psyche. These wounds can be healed with sincere, unconditional forgiveness, streaming through willing hearts that desire the deepest healing on every level of their being. An intimate, spiritual experience of radical forgiveness allows women and men to feel safe, honored, loved and respected by a trustworthy practitioner of the opposite sex. In this space of assured safety, the divine feminine or masculine can recalibrate and reemerge, reinstating the receiver's sovereign power to thrive and fully flower as a nurturing light and empowered force for good in this world. We evolve our soul's life by reclaiming our sacred birthright—original innocence.

When young women are taught to fear their bodies, fear their power, misunderstand their beauty, and discount their true feelings, the divine feminine is dishonored. When young men are taught to force their bodies, force their power, misunderstand their strength, and discount their true feelings, the divine masculine is dishonored. Modern-day mystery schools are teaching the exact opposite—to worship Mother Gaia and honor Father Sky, recognizing our place here as stewards of our beloved mother. They teach us to honor the masculine and feminine principles equally, witnessing their union as the primary principle within the dynamics of all created form. Awareness of this brings to light what is possible.

The unravelling of mistrust, betrayal, and abandonment will have a deep and powerful effect on the healing of all our relationships with everyone in our life. We can learn to apologize for blaming, projecting and holding hatred, resentment, and judgments towards others. It is wise to ask forgiveness for any hurt we may have caused to their grandfathers, grandmothers, fathers, mothers, sisters, brothers, wives, husbands, lovers, daughters, and sons.

The sacred apology is a profound tool that carries strong medicine for both the masculine and feminine counterparts within the one spirit. Often, forgiveness takes place through a dialog between the practitioner and the client. The practitioner's role is to encourage the client to identify and communicate who and what still requires forgiving.

The practitioner can offer the receiver a safe temple within which to come to terms with their most cherished wounds, accept them, forgive them, and heal them, releasing the hurtful charge that's being held within their psyche and their heart. This sacred, loving space of safety allows the hurt within a memory to be fully expressed and dissolved through a tender acceptance without any resistance.

Inside the Sacred Apology Process

Briefly, this is how the process works: First, in a healing space or temple, the practitioner goes vertical, allowing grace to descend within and around both self and receiver. Then, within a truth-dialog inquiry the receiver tells their hurtful story, and the practitioner acknowledges the hurt that has been caused. By implementing a sacred apology, the practitioner offers the receiver a chance to forgive the cherished wounds that have deep imprints in their psyche and are embedded in their guarded heart as hurtful memories.

First, the receiver will bring up and acknowledge their abuse issues verbally, laying out what they've been holding onto. When the practitioner listens carefully to a client explaining what is in their heart, the client will feel received, and tears may flow. The receiver may not remember who is at cause or exactly what took place, but the memory is locked deep within their psyche, their energy centers (chakras), and the cells of their body, perhaps causing some form of pain or disease. Many times, genetic memory has been passed down through the family lineage or carried through several lifetimes to land at the receiver's feet, for healing in this lifetime.

A healthy practitioner can facilitate a sacred apology with a traumatized receiver, revealing that the receiver too, as man or as woman, is deeply loved, appreciated, respected, and born innocent—to remain innocent and die innocent. This spiritual truth shifts the receiver's perspective out of victimhood, into self-awareness, self-responsibility, and self-healing.

When a man has a chance to fully express his deepest feelings in a sacred environment with a sensitive woman practitioner, it fosters the release of his hurtful memories and those imprinted feelings of mistrust and disrespect.

When a man has healed his inner feminine, he can access his full power with a greater understanding of what women grow through in dealing with their feelings toward spiritually immature men. All male clients should be encouraged to tune into their feminine nature, their goddess self, and practice nurturing themselves more fully. Then they will be able to live in more harmony with the rhythms and needs of the feminine life force, holding presence for her evolution.

For a female practitioner, the largest part of the sacred apology process is about learning how to fully receive the deeper feelings of a man who is emotionally wounded, as he becomes vulnerable and opens his heart to forgive his resentment towards certain women. For a male practitioner, the sacred apology process involves offering a woman an environment of assured safety and respect from within which she may fully express and come to terms with her most cherished wounds, accept them, and forgive them, while the practitioner holds a tender, loving energetic embrace for the miracle of healing to appear.

I am so very grateful that many are discovering the sacred apology and how it works. As the body of all humanity matures, the balance between the divine masculine and feminine on our planet is being restored slowly and steadily, right here and right now. In this process of transformation much arises to be forgiven. Quite often, for a substantial healing to take place, all hell will break loose before heaven can be successfully restored within each and every human soul passing through this current lifetime. We are all coming hOMe.

The next sections are purposely aimed at addressing the deeper wounds that men and women carry against each other. Divorce is one of the most common occurrences in our modern society. It is not a gender-specific process, yet there is so much unresolved resentment between the masculine and feminine psyches that this particular application of the sacred apology will be guided toward the primary roles of man to woman and woman to man. This masculine–feminine balance is the foundation of all creation—father, mother, child. The plant, animal, and human kingdoms are propagated within this universal triad. The process also works very well when a healed, conscious woman holds sacred space for another woman, and a healed, conscious man holds sacred space for another man. Just follow the protocols and trust the process. Let the holy spirit run the program for both giver and receiver and relax into the delicate process of true forgiveness.

Beyond Gender

Remember, the sacred apology is NOT a gender-specific protocol. It is a *polarity*-specific protocol. We are working to rebalance and unify polarities. A skilled practitioner may assume any role that's required to empower a healing for their receiver, whether that means allowing the ones who have passed on to speak through us to their loved one before us, or to hold the highest aspect of an opposite but inseparable polarity. The sacred apology man-to-man, or woman-to-woman, will work very well when the imagination and spirit are keen to create the specific character role of the "other" for the receiver's healing experience.

EXERCISE: The Masculine Practitioner's Role for the Feminine Receiver

This delicate forgiveness process offers a humble posture that a male practitioner can assume as a woman untangles and lets go of the cause of her suffering as well as her unhealthy reactions towards those who trigger her wounds. Her feelings of being abused (verbally, emotionally, or physically) by masculine figures in her life are imprints held within her body-mind as though they are still true for her now. Nothing could be further from the truth. It's like a footprint in the sand near the water's edge at the beach. Forgiveness technology, like a gentle wave, will wash over it and fill the imprint with fresh water (love) and sand (tiny stones of truth), smoothing the surface, as if the imprint was never there. In other words, a gentle inquiry into her story's authenticity will unlock her pain and set her free.

After the receiver has shared her abuse issues thoroughly, the practitioner can look directly into her eyes with vulnerable humility and compassion, as they begin to soul gaze, breathing and opening the spirit channel together. At this point the receiver is ready and willing to melt away any resistance coming up, and let go of her painful memories. Ask her to imagine that her abuser is sitting in front of her where you are sitting. Through you, the practitioner, he has heard her feelings and will now engage with her in the healing process.

With eyes closed, both sitting inside the hurtful memories, drawing in slow deep breaths of pure light, filling the space with divine transcendence, the practitioner can now speak to the heart of the receiver's soul, to the little girl in her, as the abuser, and ever so tenderly saying:

"I apologize for myself and every man who has ever hurt you. I apologize for all those who have caused you pain or abused you in any way, at any time, in any lifetime. We are very sorry for our actions. Please forgive us."

Having spoken these potent words with profound sincerity, the power to heal is now within *her* domain.

The timing of the sacred apology is critical. It must be delivered when her heart has opened wide enough after delivering her painful story and feeling that it's been fully received. Then she's open enough to let in these healing words and allow them fully into her tender heart, dissolving the dark, crystallized memory, allowing the waves of love and light to clean the story, washing away the imprint.

When the receiver learns to relax into witnessing her pain unravel, she will heal the cause of all her issues. The practitioner will witness the receiver's elegant management of this moment—a golden opportunity for the receiver to reclaim her power and rebuild her life on self-responsibility, self-respect, and trust for herself when she's with an unhealed masculine force. When she lets the sacred apology into her most cherished wounds the traumatic imprints within her psyche will finally dissolve, setting everyone within the painful memory free.

EXERCISE: The Feminine Practitioner's Role for the Masculine Receiver

This delicate forgiveness process offers a humble posture that a female practitioner can assume as a man untangles and lets go of the cause of his suffering as well as his unhealthy reactions towards those who trigger his wounds. His feelings of being abused (verbally, emotionally, or physically) by feminine figures in his life are imprints held within his body-mind as though they are still true for him now. Nothing could be further from the truth. It's like a footprint in the sand near the water's edge at the beach. Forgiveness technology, like a gentle wave, will wash over it and fill the imprint with fresh water (love) and sand (tiny stones of truth), smoothing the surface, as if the imprint was never there. In other words, a gentle inquiry into his story's authenticity will unlock his pain and set him free.

After the receiver has shared his abuse issues thoroughly, the practitioner can look directly into his eyes with vulnerable humility and compassion, as they begin to soul gaze, breathing and opening the spirit channel together. At this point the receiver is ready and willing to melt away any resistance coming up, and let go of his painful memories. Ask him to imagine that his abuser is sitting in front of him where you are sitting. Through you, she has heard his feelings and will now engage with him in the healing process.

With eyes closed, both sitting inside the hurtful memories, drawing in slow deep breaths of pure light, filling the space with divine transcendence, the practitioner can now speak to the heart of the receiver's soul, to the little boy in him, as the abuser, and ever so tenderly saying:

"I apologize for myself and every woman who has ever hurt you. I apologize for all those who have caused you pain or abused you in any way, at any time, in any lifetime. We are very sorry for our actions. Please forgive us."

Having spoken these potent words with profound sincerity, the power to heal is now within *his* domain.

The timing of the sacred apology is critical. It must be delivered when his heart has opened wide enough after delivering his painful story and feeling that it's been fully received. Then he's open enough to let in these healing words and allow them fully into his tender heart, dissolving the dark, crystallized memory, allowing the waves of love and light to clean the story, washing away the imprint.

When the receiver learns to relax into witnessing his pain unravel, he will heal the cause of all his issues. The practitioner will witness the receiver's elegant management of this moment—a golden opportunity for the receiver to reclaim his power and rebuild his life on self-responsibility, self-respect, and trust for himself when he's with an unhealed feminine force. When he lets the sacred apology into his most cherished wounds the traumatic imprints within his psyche will finally dissolve, setting everyone within the painful memory free.

Resolution, Integration, and Transparency

Spiritual intimacy is the golden mean by which we spiral upward into what is called enlightenment. When two spiritually mature beings engage intimately, they begin to share two overlapping radiant spirals of integrated life potential. Children born out of this union with divinity—whether they be human children, creative projects, or eco-companies—will be a powerful healing force throughout the entire universe, not just here on earth.

In the realm of healing, for a sensitive, aware, intuitive, conscious woman to experience a sensitive, aware, intuitive, conscious male pratitioner is a profound confirmation for her that kind and gentle men who can respond to her deepest need for spiritual intimacy do in fact exist. And the feminine–masculine abuse issues from our heritage will have been recalibrated once again. When any woman experiences a sacred apology for her own soul, it ripples out and affects all women as well as Mother Earth, assisting to restore the integral balance within our collective masculine–feminine matrixes.

Of course, it works both ways. For a sensitive, aware, intuitive, conscious man to experience a sensitive, aware, intuitive, conscious woman practitioner is a profound confirmation for him, that kind, deeply caring women who know how to respond to his deepest need for spiritual intimacy do in fact exist. Both giver and receiver are nourished to the core of their being. Through the spirit channel, all men everywhere will receive the rippling effect from the healing of his soul and recalibration of the integral balance within our collective masculine–feminine matrixes.

Singing, dancing, chanting, meditating, slow, deep breathing, conscious lovemaking, and praying are the best ways to access a deeper connection with our divinity, our angelic self. Daily practice in these arts helps us foster a consistent connection with our primordial light. When things seem to become emotionally unstable, when we are enveloped in dark feelings and can't seem to find our way out, if we have practiced this connection daily when things are calm it will offer us assurance that whatever we are dealing with will come and go. In the most devastating emotional storms, it is good to remember that "this too shall pass." And when cleared up, creative inspiration will have a clean, empty space to return to.

Wherever we are and whatever process we find ourself doing, alone or with someone else, we'll be able to manage it with more ease and grace when we remember to go vertical, breathe, and witness the miracle that is unfolding. Listen carefully! The voice of heaven will lead us on as we co-create a shift in perception in the entire human collective from fear to love—absolute love, divine love, immortal love—the love that we are, in a human body. God's eternal love brings a profound peace that is beyond our capacity to comprehend.

When we proclaim, "I am living God's life—as God is living my life," our walk through life will be kinder and gentler. May all beings be happy within the experience of their true essence—everlasting love—living within this physical dimension. What a phenomenal gift creation has bestowed upon us as her beloved children. Let's make the best of it and join hands in the evolution of divine love— as the maturing of all human souls slowly progresses here on earth.

Afterword

May the three books in this Sacred Apology series nurture your soul's longing for the answers of how to navigate the variety of physical experiences offered here on earth. Each of the books in this series carries the same message. They are designed to peel away the sour skin of experience so we can eat the sweet fruit of original innocence; to remove from our thinking minds the untruths that limit us; to cultivate an intimate relationship with the light of our own soul as our significant other for us to fall deeply in love with; and to find freedom from suffering.

These three books took several years to write, while I continued developing all that I am sharing with you here. After three decades of witnessing and watching the evolution of effective healing in my private practice, I chose to present to you the most effective tools and techniques that any spiritual psychologist, shamanistic healer, minister, or miracle worker can use in their own healing practice.

It is important to remember that we are never alone, no matter how alone we feel. The unseen helpers live above the horizon, so look up and talk to them, call on them and open to receive their wisdom.

I strongly encourage anyone who decides to heal to be gentle and patient with this delicate process. Some changes will be immediate and some will take lifetimes. Just don't give up! Be steadfast in your pursuit of happiness. Trust in the divine to lead you toward your next lesson and transform it into gold using all the wisdom you have cultivated through challenging experiences and all that I have shared with you here in these three volumes.

God bless you always in all ways.

About the Author

Wayne Kealohi Powell is the founder of Hawaiian Shamanic Bodywork and Global Hoʻoponopono Alliance, a vehicle for extending the power of forgiveness worldwide. He is in service as a Doctor of Divinity, holistic health educator, applied kinesiologist, author, singer-songwriter, and recording artist. He has facilitated healing courses, private sessions, and concerts in Europe, the UK, Australia, and North America.

Wayne has studied Hawaiian esoteric shamanism since 1985 and began teaching kahuna science—huna and the way of aloha—on Molokai in 1995. His work honors the many teachers, students, and musicians who helped deepen his love for all things spiritual through four decades of exploring spiritual physiology and Hawaiian culture. He is the author, with Patricia Lynn Miller, of *Hawaiian Shamanistic Healing: Medicine Ways to Cultivate the Aloha Spirit* (Llewellyn, 2018).

As a teacher and through his books, songs, and prayers Wayne's passion is to assist others to reclaim their life's power and purpose. His courses and workshops can be found at **shamanicbodywork.com** and **globalha.net**. His original music can be found at **waynepowellmusic.com**.